FIX YOUR Crown

FIX YOUR Crown

A COMPANION WORKBOOK FOR DAMAGED CROWNS STILL SHINE

LATWAINA KELLEY

Empower Outlook
LLC.

DETROIT, MI

FIX YOUR CROWN

The information in this book is based on the author's knowledge, experience, and opinions. The methods described in this book are not intended to be a definitive set of instructions. You may discover other methods and materials to accomplish the same end result. Your results may differ.

FIX YOUR CROWN © 2022 LatWaina Kelley

Paperback ISBN: 979-8-218-09410-2

Empower OutLook, LLC
Detroit, MI

Printed in the United States of America
First Edition, December 2022

Editing: Make Your Mark Publishing Solutions
Cover Design by: Make Your Mark Publishing Solutions
Interior Layout: Make Your Mark Publishing Solutions

Contents

The Queen this book belongs to is:

_____

Introduction

This workbook is the companion to my memoir, *Damaged Crowns Still Shine*. Overcoming the trauma and challenges in your life requires awareness and action, so this workbook is designed to help you work through those challenges. Inside, you'll find chapter summaries, afterthoughts, and targeted questions to help you identify patterns, weaknesses, strengths, and opportunities for growth in your life. Space is provided for you to engage in exercises by answering a series of questions after each chapter summary and afterthought.

You may find it helpful to revisit your answers along your journey of self-discovery, and your responses may change significantly along the way. If that happens, order another copy of the workbook!

It is my hope that you learn and grow upon completion of the exercises inside this workbook and you find infinite self-love and true happiness within.

Blessings,
Latwaina Kelley

"Life is one big road with lots of signs. So when you riding through the ruts, don't complicate your mind. Flee from hate. Mischief and jealousy. Don't bury your thoughts, put your vision to reality. Wake up and live."

~Bob Marley

Beginnings

Recall Summary & Afterthought

Chapter 1 gives us an up close and personal look into my childhood. While I was loved and doted on by my father, my relationship with my mother was far from the same. In fact, it was nearly opposite. The youngest of three, I grew up around immediate and extended family members, but somehow appeared invisible to them. It set the tone for what followed throughout my childhood.

As Chapter 1 reveals, family dynamics set the tone for what goes on both inside and outside the house. In economics, it's called infrastructure, and it determines the strength of the economy. In the family dynamic, a weak infrastructure is a root of some form of physical, mental, or psychological instability. The introduction of drugs and/or alcohol are sure to disrupt family dynamics, leading to stress, tension, and conflict.

My early experiences serve as a perfect model for how dysfunction can hijack a normal childhood. For children, there's a deafening silence when physical abuse occurs. We hear it, but we don't; some of us even tune it out. Nevertheless, the longer it continues, the more damage it does to those in the family. Eventually, things will begin to unravel, like it did in my life. Each affected family member can deal with the situation differently. One child may divert their attention to a hobby such as reading, writing, playing an instrument, or fixing electronics, for instance; another child might become closed off and withdrawn, keeping to themselves. These are clear signs that the change in the family dynamic is having a negative effect on the children. Even if the behavior "appears" positive, if it is an altered behavior pattern, it's time to seek help. Remember, children are not equipped to solicit the help and resources they need. It is up to the adults to look out for the children in the village.

CHAPTER 1

Workbook Questions

1. Can you recall an incident that occurred in your youth that caused you to feel invisible or like you had little to no voice? Describe what happened.

2. How did it make you feel?

   Check all that apply:

   ☐ Sad
   ☐ Embarrassed
   ☐ Angry
   ☐ Resentful
   ☐ Withdrawn

3. Do you think the experience shaped your personality? If so, how? (examples: it made you extroverted, introverted, shy, etc.) Please explain.

....

....

....

....

....

....

....

....

....

....

....

....

4. Have you ever spoken to the other person/people involved about this incident? If not, why?

....

....

....

....

....

....

....

5. Have you healed from this incident?

....

....

....

....

....

....

....

....

Keeping Secrets

Recall Summary & Afterthought

Chapter 2 delves deeper into the dynamics of my family. The ole adage, "What goes on in this house stays in this house" is akin to poison from the most venomous snakes. When I innocently revealed what was going on in the home, I was immediately reprimanded for it. My mother, Grace, repeated that same damaging and manipulative statement, and that was when I learned to keep dark secrets, even when it was detrimental to my own well-being.

It's important to note that forcing children to keep secrets is one of the most dangerous things adults can do. It sets the precedent for predators to target their innocence. We groom children to keep secrets when we forbid them to divulge trouble or the secrets of the adults in the home. They get used to it. And by the time the predator threatens them or convinces them that they're unwanted or that inappropriate touching should be kept secret, there is little resistance from the child. Why? Because the adults have already groomed the child into thinking that keeping secrets, no matter how big or small, is normal. We must realize that forcing children to keep secrets, even our own dirty discretions, is like preventing children from breathing.

While it's true that everyone wants some measure of privacy, the balance between privacy and secrecy must be carefully weighed when children are involved. After all, in the end, truth finds its way from beneath the covers, behind the curtains and closed doors, and between the walls. There are many Latwaina's in the world. You might be "Latwaina" in the sense that you've harbored harrowing secrets that have kept your soul captive. The questions that follow may help you identify whether you've been a victim and help you release yourself from this perpetual form of bondage.

CHAPTER 2

Workbook Questions

1. Are there any secrets in your family? If so, list them.

....

....

....

....

....

....

2. Does anybody ever openly talk about these secrets? Yes / No

   If not, why not?

....

....

....

....

....

....

3. What would you say are some of the effects of keeping family secrets?

....
....
....
....
....
....
....
....

4. How can the harm caused by keeping family secrets be avoided or minimized (at a minimum)?

....
....
....
....
....
....
....
....
....
....

Target Practice

Recall Summary & Afterthought

If you've ever been in the military or gone to the gun range to practice shooting, you are familiar with target practice. Target practice is an exercise in which weapons are shot at a target. The purpose of target practice is to improve the aim or the handling expertise of the person firing the weapon. It's the preliminary step to the "real thing." The ammunition used in target practice will not cause the same type or amount of damage that is caused by defense rounds, or "real bullets." Sexual predators most often engage in target practice just as Uncle Nick did with me. It starts with subtle gestures, like an inappropriate compliment, an inappropriate touch, graduating to coercion, then forced encounters like the ride to the store, and being omnipresent or seemingly always around. These are all forms of target practice that occur before the predator advances to a more gruesome form of sexual violence against his or her victim.

Target practice allows the predator to assess his or her victims: *Are they fearful? Will they tell? Can I manipulate them?* And it's not just limited to sexual encounters. It's through target practice that the predator perfects their skills to manipulate, harass, intimidate, coerce, belittle, etc. It almost always precedes a full-scale attack or encounter, as it happened with me. If we can recognize these patterns, we just might be able to stop sexual predators dead in their tracks.

CHAPTER 3
Workbook Questions

1. Thinking back, can you identify any situations in which you believe you were being used as "target practice" for a negative experience or encounter? If so, please describe it (you do not have to include names).

....

....

....

....

....

....

....

....

....

....

....

....

....

....

2. Have you ever suspected that someone you know was/is being set up to be a victim in a "target practice" scenario?

3. How would you see yourself intervening if you witnessed or suspected someone was being targeted like I was in the story?

4. Do you possess any characteristics/traits that you believe could make you appear vulnerable to someone like Uncle Nick?

5. Do you have an "Uncle Nick" in your family or community?

"If God is for you, who can be against you?"

~Romans 8:31

The Lion's Den

Recall Summary & Afterthought

The term "lion's den" refers to a place or state in which you are at an tremendous disadvantage or face extreme hostility. In these situations, it is easy for you to cave in and become vulnerable prey to the lions. Let's face it, we have all found ourselves in the lion's den at some point in our lives. It doesn't mean you have faced sexual assault as I have. In your case, it might have been a different scenario altogether. But whenever you're in the lion's den, you likely believe you only have two choices—fight or flight. But it's not that easy. The lion in your life represents the predator who is out to get you. It doesn't have to be an Uncle Nick (someone looking to rape you); the lion in your life can be anyone who is looking to do harm to you, be it physical or emotional.

Think about how lions catch their prey. It's rather profound. The lion's prey isn't always caught off guard. In many instances, the prey sees the lion but is unable to escape. Once the lion has its eyes set on its target, it stays laser focused and waits for the opportune time to attack—when the prey has perfect positioning. The lion is successful at catching its prey when it can bite its neck and crush its windpipe, causing suffocation. At the same time, the lion uses its claws to wound its prey. Therefore, even if the prey just happens to get away, the severe wounds the lion inflicted will cause the prey to eventually die. The key here is for the prey to stay in a position that makes it impossible for the lion to inflict deadly harm.

How does this relate to you? None of us decide that we want to be vulnerable prey. Sometimes, it comes out of nowhere. You are stalked. You are attacked verbally. You are used as a scapegoat. You are ostracized. You are criticized. But you must come into the awareness that you, like the lion's prey, must maintain a firm position, one that will not allow you to become a victim to the lion in your life. As a thirteen-year-old, I was vulnerable and didn't know how to maintain a physical and psychological posture that wouldn't allow me to succumb to Uncle Nick's attacks, my family, and the bad boyfriends I became involved with. For this reason, I remained in the lion's den. However, today, I am no longer being held captive, and I maintain a posture that will not allow me to be taken down by the lions in my life. And trust me, there are plenty of them.

Finally, think about the lions in your life. Who are they? How can you avoid them? And how can you maintain a posture that prevents you from being taken down by the lions in your life?

CHAPTER 4

Workbook Questions

1. Have you ever been in the lion's den when it comes to your family/friends or close associates?

2. When you consider the Afterthought for The Lion's Den, can you relate to possessing the traits of the predator, the prey, or both? Explain.

3. If you can relate to the prey (being in a position to be attacked), are you able to decipher what that position is? In other words, when are you most vulnerable? Is it when you're experiencing depression, isolation, loneliness, heartache?

....

....

....

....

....

....

....

4. How can you maintain a posture that prevents you from being taken down by the lions in your life?

....

....

....

....

....

....

....

Double Trauma

Recall Summary & Afterthought

Why God allows us to experience tragedy can seem like an eternal mystery. The reality is, however, some painful things can never be explained or understood. This truth can cause us to continuously lament in sorrow and discouragement. But it's fascinating to know that in some of our lowest moments in life, we can find solace. Picking up the pieces of your life after trauma can seem daunting. But this is where courage and strength spring up from within. In fact, finding consolation and comfort in yourself and your own thoughts is a strength in itself.

Some may not believe this, but my life is a testament that you can, indeed, find solace or comfort in your sorrow. In some of your deepest and darkest days, a simple word or phrase or even Scripture can be the spiritual food you need to pick yourself up, dust yourself off, and keep striving forward. Strength and courage are already inside us, but they can lie dormant until we summon them forth. And sometimes, it's only through hardships and trials that we discover what truly lies deep within us—*power*. We have power to overcome anything in life, except death. Look at how phenomenal and powerful God made us!

I believe Psalms 147:3 – "He healeth up the broken in heart, and bindeth up their wounds." Scripture is powerful; it's the uttered Word of God through man. Just like this book, it is God-ordained to spread God's love, His promises, and His healing power. There's no way I could have overcome the double tragedy in my life without God having a hand in it. You can find comfort in sorrow, tap into your internal reservoir, and unveil a monumental reserve where courage, strength, and forgiveness all dwell.

CHAPTER 5

Workbook Questions

1. Have you ever experienced peace when you were dead smack in the middle of the worst mess (chaos)? Describe the situation.

....

....

....

....

....

....

2. If so, what did you do?

....

....

....

....

....

....

....

....

....

3. What do you typically do when you find yourself in a chaotic situation?

    ....

    ....

    ....

    ....

    ....

    ....

    ....

    ....

4. Do you have a favorite Scripture or quote that you read or recite when you are dealing
    with chaotic situations? Is so, write it out below.

    ....

    ....

    ....

    ....

    ....

    ....

    ....

    ....

5. The Summary & Afterthought for this chapter references the internal reservoir we all have and can tap into when needed. What are the contents of your internal reservoir? What do you think might be missing from it?

....

....

....

....

....

....

....

....

....

....

....

....

....

....

Changing Places ... Trading Spaces

Recall Summary & Afterthought

Chapter 6 provides a visual for the impacts moving can have on the family. While moving can be exciting, as it was for my family, especially my mother, Grace, the emotion that comes from moving to a new environment can be overwhelming. In fact, it can turn a supposedly positive scenario into a negative scenario. Changing physical locations doesn't always mean a bed of roses awaits the move. You see, if you haven't dumped emotional baggage, it just follows you to the next location. Hence, the terminology, "Trading Spaces." This is what occurred in my case. I was so used to keeping secrets, hiding my shame, and burying my emotions that there was no way that simply moving from one location to another was going to lead to a positive experience.

While moving may seem comforting, initially, all problems soon find us, as they did with my mother and me. Why? Because as we see, change must come from within first. Running away from my problems gave me a false sense of comfort—that the monsters no longer existed or that I had escaped the circumstances I'd found myself in. Truthfully, however, the monsters were still present, and my circumstances didn't change.

As I learned, running away from your problems is a race that you can never win. Because one day, no matter how long it's been or how far away you move, you are going to have to face your Goliaths. You must fix them. And fixing them means shifting your mindset. Problems serve a purpose in our lives. They mature us. They exercise our mental muscles. They give us stamina and endurance ... something a physical location, alone, could never do.

CHAPTER 6

Workbook Questions

1. Have you moved away (from one physical location to another) in an effort to distance yourself from a certain person, situation, or environment? If so, what happened afterward? Did you reap the desired result? Please provide details.

....

....

....

....

....

....

2. Do you consider distancing yourself from a negative experience running from your problems?

....

....

....

....

....

....

....

3. Do you believe facing the giants in your life is the best course of action? Why or why not?

....

....

....

....

....

....

....

4. How might you deal with a difficult person or experience differently?

....

....

....

....

....

....

....

....

5. Do you have an exit strategy for dealing with difficult situations, be they at work, school, church, within the family structure, etc.?

All David had was faith and a rock to defeat his giant.
All you need is faith in a rock to defeat yours.
"The Lord is my rock. My fortress. My deliverer."

~Psalms 182

David Versus Goliath

Recall Summary & Afterthought

You don't have to be a devout Catholic or a Bible-thumping Christian to be familiar with the story of David and Goliath. In fact, most of us probably learned of the story in grade school. And because one should never assume that everyone knows the story, I summarize it briefly.

David was a young shepherd boy, as they called him. Essentially, he took care of sheep in his father's pasture. Biblical scholars and historians describe him as scrawny, or tiny … somebody most people wouldn't fear. The Israelites, which was David's lineage, learned that their opposing enemy, the Philistines, were preparing to invade their territory and they began to prepare. While his eleven brothers left for war, David was left behind. In their mind, the scrawny little dude was of no real value to beating the great Philistine army. But when the two armies gathered to stand on opposite sides of a deep valley, a Philistine giant named Goliath that stood over nine feet tall came to the front of the Philistine battle line. For forty days, Goliath took his post and mocked the Israelites and their God. Goliath called to them to fight, but King Saul and the Israelites were too afraid of Goliath and his intimidating stature.

At some point, David was sent by his father to see what was going on with the war and provide an update. Imagine David's surprise when he arrived on war grounds and discovered the Israelites cowering with fear. David just had to get involved. He persuaded the king to allow him to fight in the war. There was only one problem: David didn't have the proper weaponry. But with his sling, he gathered five smooth stones. Now imagine what the nine-foot giant was thinking. He probably bellowed over with laughter. Drawing his sword and spear, he attempted to take David out. But the young boy placed his stones in the sling and launched a startling attack at the giant, bringing him down and killing him. This caused the Philistine army to retreat.

Imagine the cheers and accolades from soldiers in the Israelite army. Imagine their astonishment. This is a reflection of what is done or can be done in our lives. There is no giant—be it a problem, a job, a boss, a coworker, a troubled marriage, addiction, unruly children, you name it—that is too big for the David in you. You are equipped with courage that is waiting to be unleashed. I've faced my share of Goliaths. And guess what … I'm not done. I'm pretty sure I'll face many more throughout the remainder of my life. But one thing I know for sure; I have good aim. I can take out the Goliaths in my life. Just give me the sling and a few smooth stones.

Take a few tips from chapter:

1. *Be bigger than your fears.*
2. *Size doesn't matter.*
3. *You are already equipped with the tools of survival, so use them.*
4. *Never underestimate your skills and capabilities.*
5. *Be like David!*

Workbook Questions

1. Is there a Goliath in your life right now? Describe the situation.

....

....

....

....

....

....

2. How are you dealing with your Goliath situation? If you don't have a current "Goliath" in your life, you can reference a past situation when you found yourself facing a "Goliath."

....

....

....

....

....

....

3. Do you believe you can defeat the Goliath in your life? How?

....

....

....

....

....

....

....

....

4. What do you think the purpose of Goliath is in your life? Do you think it's there to build your faith, your endurance, your confidence, etc.?

....

....

....

....

....

....

....

....

....

5. What is on the other side of your Goliath situation? Is there peace, victory, normalcy?

Bits and Pieces

Recall Summary & Afterthought

Chapter 8 is a reminder that people who are unimportant to you cross your life; they touch it in one way or the other and move on. There are people who cause you to breathe a sigh of relief when they leave you and make you wonder why you ever encountered them. There are people who make you breathe a sigh of remorse when they leave you and have you wondering why they had to go and leave such a gaping hole. This phenomenon is referred to as the "bits and pieces of life."

As we see in this chapter, I spent a good deal of time "sweating the small stuff," some of which, in the grand scheme of things, were miniscule. What I didn't initially realize was what I thought was meant to hurt me was actually meant to help me mature and grow. Even when my emotions became aroused from embarrassment, humiliation, jealousy, or shame, they were bits and pieces of a greater plan. Even though I wanted to end my life, if I had succeeded, I would have experienced a premature death. Why? Because it wasn't my time to die. I was meant to live. Bowing out or ending your life might seem like the right thing to do when you're experiencing pain, but as I've shown with my story, there is so much more to live for on the other side of pain. Pain is temporary. It doesn't last always. It's just a piece of the puzzle of life.

Children leave parents. Friends leave friends. Acquaintances move on. People change homes. People grow apart. Enemies hate and move on. Friends love and move on. Think of the many people who have moved into your hazy memory. Look at those who are present and wonder. We are all people who move in and out of each other's lives, each one leaving his or her mark on the other. You'll find you are made up of bits and pieces of all who ever touched your life, and you are more because of it. You would be different if they had not connected with you or touched you in some way, shape, or form.

Our lives are not made up of a single moment in time. Rather, it is made up of several moments that, in the bigger scheme of things, seem more like bits and pieces. But that's the beauty and magic of thinking of life like a kaleidoscope. When you look back over your life and take inventory, you will find you are made up of bits and pieces of the good and the bad. Sometimes, however, it is not always easy to see or accept this notion, especially when you've experienced hurt, trauma, rejection, and abandonment.

To the contrary, sometimes, we can be too focused on the bits and pieces and fail to realize that there is a bigger picture. Herein, we must remember to have balance. These things go together. You can't create a puzzle without putting the bits and pieces together. You'll never be able to view the picture that the complete puzzle reveals if you stay focused on the bits and pieces. But without bits and pieces there is no puzzle. Your life is the completed puzzle, made up of tiny episodes in your life, beautiful moments, sad moments, and sometimes, hurtful moments. Remember, your life is too important to think about ending it at your own hands. You would interrupt the completion of the puzzle of your life.

If you or someone you know has thoughts of committing suicide, please contact the National Suicide Prevention Lifeline at 1-800-273-8255 or through online chats at https://suicide-preventionlifeline.org/chat/. Counselors provide suicide prevention and mental health crisis assistance.

CHAPTER 8

Workbook Questions

1. Do you believe the concept of your life being or becoming a kaleidoscope?

....
....
....
....
....
....
....

2. What does the puzzle in your life look like? Are there missing pieces?

....
....
....
....
....
....
....

3. What do you want the final puzzle of your life to look like?

....

....

....

....

....

....

....

....

4. Do you believe you can influence the shape and design of your life? If so, how?

....

....

....

....

....

....

....

....

A Chance at Love

Recall Summary & Afterthought

Love is about taking risks.

There are many opinions about whether taking risks for love is a good or terrible idea, but in the end, that doesn't even matter. Fear is the most powerful weapon on earth, whether it be fear of being hurt, being ridiculed, making mistakes, failing, or not reaching our goal. Fear can stop us from achieving or dreams, our goals, or even stop us from taking chances on people who want the best for us. If we keep hiding from love, we'll only hurt ourselves and others. As I showed in Chapter 9, for my old wounds to heal, I needed to give myself a chance to let someone help me heal them. I had to open myself up to love as well as other choices that proved to help me grow. If the love lasts for ten months or ten years, it's still love in its purest form, and it does what love is supposed to do—help us grow. Love is powerful, but when we are afraid to take the chance at love, we rob ourselves of the most indescribable feeling in the world.

My story also shows that love teaches us more about ourselves than any other emotion. We cannot learn from fear because it paralyzes our actions and heightens our emotions. We may say that love didn't work out when our relationships fail or end. But that's not necessarily true. There are positive byproducts of love, and offspring is one of them. I took a chance at love, and it brought me a beautiful daughter. The birth of my daughter showed me what unconditional love is all about. Had it not been for me taking the risk to love, I would have stayed paralyzed in fear, with feelings of betrayal, hurt, and shame.

Remember, it all starts with a choice, and this time, the choice is to open your heart and let others know the real you as I was brave enough to do.

Let the world know you for who you really are, not who you want the world to think you are. Go ahead and love. Risk it all, take chances, get hurt, get back up, and try it again.

And never let fear stop you from opening your heart to that person who is ready to make sacrifices for you. Love is a two-way feeling, so if you take risks by opening your heart, remember that someone else is taking the same risk by letting you know who they really are … good or bad. My story shows that risks are challenging and they're scary, but the feeling of overcoming your fears and achieving your goals is indescribable. And when we overcome them for love, it's even better.

As we all eventually discover, love is a journey, and we receive fragments of love as we travel the path of life. Ultimately, we must love ourselves before we can love anyone else in a healthy way. If we don't, we will remain in a perpetual cycle of dealing with the negative consequences of love.

CHAPTER 9

Workbook Questions

1. Have you ever risked loving someone? Please provide details.

2. Do you believe love involves risk?

3. What is your perspective/view on failed relationships? Do you believe they provide any value? Why or why not?

4. In your opinion, does love ever involve hurt or pain? Explain your position.

5. What is the greatest lesson love has taught you?

Love Lessons

Recall Summary & Afterthought

Chapter 10 is one of the most powerful chapters in *Damaged Crowns Still Shine* because it illustrates the power of love. You see, in love, we do not make mistakes, but we do learn lessons. I took a chance at love by moving beyond my hurt and pain and allowing myself to love Chad freely. Some people may think young people can't learn from love; however, they couldn't be more wrong. There is no statutory age or maturity level one must possess to become a recipient of the lessons love teaches. As I experienced, rehearsing what goes wrong in love only prolongs pain and the moving-on process. Accept what happens, good or bad, and move forward. If not, love automatically sets you up for the next lesson. As I discovered, love has lessons to give. It's love's purpose. As Chapter 10 illustrates, the lessons love teaches us helps us mature and grow.

Below is a list of lessons that Chapter 10 highlights

1. **Love is less of a feeling but more of a choice.** At first, it could be all about having butterflies when we see the person we love. This usually happens during the infatuation phase. But when we start to really love someone, when things are getting difficult and when we see their imperfections, love is about making a choice to be with that person through the challenges. Love is the reason we accept someone and why we continue to love someone despite his or her flaws.

2. **Love can never and should never be forced.** Sometimes when we are enamored with someone, we want him or her to love us in return. The more someone pulls away, the more we try to win him or her over. But love does not work that way. A forced love will never be worth it because we will only lose ourselves by trying hard to make someone love us. This is not the kind of love we deserve. Likewise, we don't need to please someone to see how good we are. No one is worth begging for.

3. **We accept the love we think we deserve.** Just because we love someone, it doesn't mean he or she should disrespect us, lie, or cheat. And just because we love someone so much, it doesn't mean he or she is the right person for us. We deserve the kind of love that is built on honesty, respect, and trust. We know we have found the right person if he or she knows our worth, cares about us, and has our best interests as their priority.

4. **We cannot love someone truly without loving ourselves.** This is the mother of all love clichés. Some people take this lesson lightly, as the chapter reveals, but if we don't love ourselves enough, we act insecurely and we accept less than what we deserve. Our love and respect for ourselves sets the bar for the kind of love and respect we receive from our significant others. Likewise, our relationship with ourselves is the only relationship that will last for our entire lifetime, and it is more important than any relationship we could have with someone else.

5. **We don't have to change ourselves for someone to like us.** No matter how much we want to change for someone, it will never work out. We need someone who will appreciate our great qualities and accept our flaws. We are perfectly fine just being ourselves, and we must believe that the person who deserves us will see that. The right person will realize that we are imperfect, but they will still love us anyway.

6. **Love must do its perfect work.** Love is the charge that helps us mature and grow. The lessons from love can be applied to other nonromantic relationships and circumstances in our lives. The lessons love teach are powerful, long lasting, and God ordained.

CHAPTER 10

Workbook Questions

1. Do you believe that love is the most powerful emotion humans can experience? Why or why not?

   ....

   ....

   ....

   ....

   ....

   ....

2. Do you believe you can love someone without loving yourself first?

   ....

   ....

   ....

   ....

   ....

   ....

   ....

3. Does love need to be reciprocated to be effective?

....

....

....

....

....

....

....

....

4. Does love involve sacrifice? How so?

....

....

....

....

....

....

....

....

5. Have you ever been manipulated through a warped view of love? If so, how? If not, why not? Explain how one can be manipulated by a warped view of love.

"When I look back over my life, I see
pain, mistakes, and heartaches.
When I look in the mirror, I see strength,
learnt lessons, and pride in myself."

~Tiny Buddha

A Love Worth Living For

Recall Summary & Afterthought

If you can recall, in Chapter 11, I was faced with living with the repercussions of my decisions. And part of the challenge was that I found myself in an adult situation. I was going to be a mother. That meant I was responsible for the well-being of another human being. And while it was exciting on one hand, it was also overwhelming on the other. I was not an adult. This meant I didn't have the arsenal to deal with the hardships of life. I was not equipped to deal with the physical nor emotional ramifications of my decision … my risk to love. In the end, I had no choice but to grow up, as much as I could reasonably grow in nine months. A tiny human being was coming into the world, and I was responsible for her.

What is interesting about this chapter is that we can look at what transpired in more than one way. If you look back on your life, you will often realize that many of the times you thought you were being rejected from something good, you were, in fact, being redirected to something better. You can't control everything. Sometimes, you just need to relax and have faith that things will work out. Let go a little and just let life happen. Because sometimes, the things you can't change end up changing you and helping you grow.

Here are a few truths about how circumstances change us for the better.

1. **Everything is as it should be.** You always end up where you're meant to be. Even tragic and stressful situations eventually teach you things you never dreamed you were going to learn. Remember, oftentimes, when things are seemingly falling apart, they are actually falling into place.

2. **Not until you are lost in this world can you begin to find your true self.** Realizing you are lost is the first step to living the life you want. The second step is leaving the life you don't want. Making a big life change is pretty scary. But you know what's even scarier? Regret. Vision without action is a daydream, and action without vision is a nightmare. Your heart is free; have the courage to follow it.

3. **Usually the deepest pain empowers you to grow to your full potential.** It's the scary, stressful choices that end up being the most worthwhile. Without pain, there would be no change. But remember, pain, just like everything in life, is meant to be learned from and then released.

You Gave Me Life – A Poem to My Children

Just when the storm began to rage, you came into my life.
Your presence alone filled me with joy, not strife.
Looking into your eyes, I made a promise to push past my pain.
For with you and God, I knew I had much more to gain.
I knew that we wouldn't always have sunny days,
but joy would be released and could no longer stay at bay.
I opened my eyes and swallowed all pride.
But God above to be my one and only guide.
I was sure I'd get some things wrong in caring for you.
But rest assured, I was sure to get some things right too!
You see, before you were born,
my heart endured the pain of being torn.
I didn't want to live to see the sun rise yet another day.
But God said, "No, my child. You must stay."
So, I dried my eyes and stood my ground,
vowing I'd chase the devil like a hound.
In my womb, you were formed,
while in my life, I was going through my storm.
I carried you with abundant love and prideful joy
because it didn't matter whether you were a girl or a boy.
My life changed the moment I gave birth;
I had a greater sense of purpose and worth.
Thank you, daughter … Thank you, son.
You gave me life, joy, and a great measure of love and fun.

4. **Some people will lie to you to get what they want.** Remember, an honest enemy is better than a friend who lies. Pay less attention to what people say and more attention to what they do. Their actions will show you the truth, which will help you measure the true quality of your relationship in the long-term.

5. **Everything is going to be all right ... eventually.** There will be times when it seems like everything that could possibly go wrong is going wrong. And you might feel like you will be stuck in this rut forever, but you won't. Sure, the sun stops shining sometimes, and you may get a huge thunderstorm or two, but eventually, the sun will come out to shine. Sometimes, it's just a matter of us walking through the storm and holding our heads up high, as I ultimately did in Chapter 11.

CHAPTER 11

Workbook Questions

1. List five things you believe are worth living for?

....

....

....

....

....

....

....

2. Do you believe we can live without someone loving us?

....

....

....

....

....

....

....

....

3. What is your interpretation of this statement: "Not until you are lost in this world can you begin to find your true self"?

....

....

....

....

....

....

....

....

4. What is your interpretation of this statement: "Usually the deepest pain empowers you to grow to your full potential"?

....

....

....

....

....

....

....

....

5. What is your interpretation of this statement: "Everything is going to be all right ... eventually"?

Gone Too Soon

Recall Summary & Afterthought

In the midst of trying to put my life back together, I received devastating news. My father was tragically killed in a car accident on New Year's morning. This tragedy couldn't have come at a more inopportune time. But is there ever a perfect time for tragedy to hit home? No, there never is. The suddenness of losing my father had a profound effect on me in more ways than one. The loss of a parent at a young age ushers in long-term emotional trauma that can be unrecognizable at first. You can't really pinpoint the source of the trauma that bleeds over into other areas of your life. For me, trying to navigate life as a young, single parent of two small children was stressful in itself. Factor in the monumental loss of my father, who was my strongest support system, and it was the perfect storm for sheer and complete disaster. However, the loss of my father set me up for what was to transpire in the coming days, weeks, months, and even years.

Although I was a "daddy's girl," I still had somewhat of a complex relationship with my father. So many of us have complex relationships with our parents—and some of us don't have one at all. Unresolved emotions like anger and resentment have a lasting effect on our psyche. The death of a parent means there is no hope of reconciliation or having your feelings validated. Perhaps this is what happened to me, setting the precedent for my relationships with men. It is plausible that I was trying to fill the void in my life due to the loss of my father when it came to men. As the story unveils, there is no substitute for a mother or father, no matter how good or bad our relationship is with them. Chances are, I was unaware that the loss of my father would profoundly and permanently alter me—mentally, physically, and emotionally—for the rest of my life. There is, however, a final takeaway from this chapter. On the other side of pain lies joy. Within days of burying my father, I officially became a homeowner. Although the process had started previously, the timing of the closing and receiving the keys to my own home were divinely set.

CHAPTER 12
Workbook Questions

1. Have you ever lost a parent or someone close to you?

    ....

    ....

    ....

    ....

    ....

    ....

2. Did you have an estranged relationship with your loved one? And if so, how has your life changed since their passing?

    ....

    ....

    ....

    ....

    ....

    ....

    ....

3. Is there something you could have done differently while that person was alive?

4. If you could spend one last day with your loved one, would you? What would you say and/or do?

5. How has your life changed since the passing of your loved one?

Money Still Can't Buy Love

Recall Summary & Afterthought

Money can't buy love. You've heard the saying a million times. But it's more than just an aged-old cliché; it's a powerful statement and painful lesson to learn. You see, many people have inadvertently tested the theory, only to find out that it still holds true, no matter how you twist or turn it.

Jamel shows up in Chapter 13 of *Damaged Crowns Still Shine.* He was attentive, caring, and good looking, things that piqued my interest. No doubt, while hurting over the loss of my father, yo-yoing in a not-so-good relationship with my mother, dealing with broken relationships with the fathers of my children and fractured relationships with most of the members of my family, including my siblings, I was in a fragile state of mind. To my rescue (or so I thought) entered a handsome so-called Christian young man named Jamel. The fact that Jamel took a liking to me sold me from day one. And I was willing to go far to keep Jamel close by, even though I initially saw red flags. But against my better judgment, I took the bait. Before it was said and done, Jamel had used me for his needs—money and sex. He even got a car out of the deal. I, in my desperate search to fill the void from the loss of my father, wanted to prove to others that I could get a man … and a good-looking one too. And I wanted to prove to myself that I was worthy of some form of love, but I got taken for all my money in the process. I was left, once again, with a broken heart. I had to pick up the pieces of my life and build myself yet again.

Chapter 13 is a vivid reminder that love is not expensive. You don't have to pay for someone's love. This lesson is simple—There is no charge for love; the best things in life are FREE!

CHAPTER 13

Workbook Questions

1. Have you ever tried to buy someone's love?

....

....

....

....

....

....

....

2. If so, what was the outcome?

....

....

....

....

....

....

....

....

3. What circumstances do you believe led you to try to buy love?

....

....

....

....

....

....

....

4. Why, in your opinion, does money not buy love?

....

....

....

....

....

....

....

5. What lesson has your experience with either trying to buy love or witnessing someone else trying to buy love taught you?

"Your crown has been bought and paid
for. Put it on your head and wear it."

~Dr. Maya Angelou

From Bad to Worse

Recall Summary & Afterthought

As if getting played by a two-timing so-called Christian gigolo wasn't bad enough, my life began to spiral out of control. From losing my full-time job to eventually losing my home, things went from bad to worse for me.

Chapter 14 signifies a wilderness experience. Some people refer to this time as a stripping process. You seemingly begin to lose everything you've worked hard to achieve. This was true for me. I began to lose everything, from my money, to my job, and my home. Not only those things, but I also began to lose my faith and confidence. With my back against the wall, I reached out to my estranged family members to request assistance.

I did what many women do—I decided to confront the culprit who had taken advantage of me. Well, of course, I didn't get the response I wanted. Jamel didn't show an ounce of remorse for what he had done. Even though it might seem like it was another epic fail, it was quite the opposite. It was a lesson I had to learn. As painful as the experience was, I had no other alternative but to learn and GROW from the experience. Whether I knew it at the time or not, I was being set up for something greater.

Things continued to spiral out of control when I lost my job. It had a domino effect. The loss of income caused me to lose my vehicle and my home—things I had worked hard to obtain. Fearing becoming homeless, I contacted my brother to ask him if my children and I could come live with him temporarily. He, however, politely and without remorse, turned me down. Then I reached out to my mother and stepfather to ask for assistance. Once again, I was turned down. Helpless and hopeless, I finally turned to the only person I could count on—Latwaina.

I reached a crossroad in Chapter 14. The greatest takeaway from the chapter is the discovery that we possess monumental strength and determination. We possess the inner ability to weather any storm and come out as a conqueror.

CHAPTER 14

Workbook Questions

1. What do you do when things go wrong in your life?

....

....

....

....

....

....

....

2. Have you ever thought God was punishing you when you experienced the loss of material possessions?

....

....

....

....

....

....

....

3. Did you lose faith after losing a material possession(s)?

4. Where you able to recover your losses? How so?

5. What did your comeback season look like? Did you receive double for your trouble or even greater blessings?

A Blessing or a Curse

Recall Summary & Afterthought

Sometimes, in our quest to bounce back from setbacks in life, we take it upon ourselves to "speed the process up." What we fail to consider is divine timing. Things may seem to be going well, but in the end, we can end up enduring another painful experience. And this is precisely what I faced in Chapter 15.

After feeling used and abused from the relationship with Jamel and subsequently losing my job, home, and car, I was determined to bounce back. Internally, I told my self that I deserved better and even that I knew better. Better than who? Better than God. I joined a dating site to seek some sense of normalcy in my life. What I failed to recognize was that the resources I was seeking came with a price tag, an expensive one too. The price tag was my body, my time, energy, and self-esteem. I didn't recognize this at first. You see, I thought the financial help I received was a blessing, and I never considered the fact that it could turn out to be a curse in the end.

Why didn't I understand this premise? Because I was too close to the experience and my pain was so fresh that I was emotionally numb. As the chapter illustrates, only the passage of time provides the perspective to discern the patterns in my life. It was only then that I was able to interpret what had happened or was happening in my life, either as a blessing or a curse.

CHAPTER 15

Workbook Questions

1. Has there ever been anything in your life you believed was a blessing, but it turned out to be a curse? Describe the situation.

....

....

....

....

....

....

....

2. When did the "blessing" become a curse?

....

....

....

....

....

....

....

....

3. What was the outcome?

4. How can you determine if something is a blessing or a curse?

5. How can you avoid falling into the blessing-turned-curse trap in the future?

Leopards Never Change Their Spots

Recall Summary & Afterthought

As we can see in this chapter, I was changing. I was not an "innocent" young woman anymore. Life had shown me how tough it can be. Unfortunately, I started learning that lesson at a young age. But I was also growing up … learning some of the secrets of the trade. That is, how to use my feminine wiles to get what I needed. After all, in my mind, it was all about survival—for me and my children.

I had a "special" arrangement with my landlord, whom I'd met on the dating site. I didn't like him, but he had something I needed. I had to appease him, which I tried to do. I even met Jeff, who I'd decided to date as well. Jeff also had what I needed—money, support, and companionship. But Jeff wanted something from me too. Sex. I found myself in a web of confusion. The bottom line is that leopards (men, in this case) do not change their spots. I was having a repeat experience because I had engaged in repeat behavior. I, too, was a leopard.

What it takes to reverse course from this type of behavior and experience starts with a changed mindset. As we can see, it doesn't happen overnight; it is a process. For me, recognizing that both my mindset and my behavior must change, was the first step in the right direction. Chapter 16 served as a mirror for me, when I performed an honest evaluation of myself.

CHAPTER 16

Workbook Questions

1. Can you spot a leopard?

....

....

....

....

....

....

2. What are the key traits to look for in leopards?

....

....

....

....

....

....

....

3. Do you have any leopards in your life? If so, how do you interact (or deal) with them?

4. Can anything positive come out of interacting with a "leopard" on an ongoing basis?

5. What, if any, purpose do leopards serve in our lives?

"Part of the healing process is sharing
with other people who care."

~Jerry Cantrell

Situationship

Recall Summary & Afterthought

Situationship. That's what I called it. A situationship is a romantic or sexual relationship that is not formal or established. For me, it was that and a web of deception and confusion that I had spun for myself. Out of desperation to keep a roof over my head and money in my pocket, I was stuck between appeasing two men whom I didn't like. One, I needed to appease for shelter and the other, to sustain my daily needs.

With most situationships, one party is more committed than the other, and it's the more committed party that is more emotionally drawn in and gets the short end of the stick. In my case, the more committed persons were Charles (a.k.a Robert) and Jeff. And like most situationships, it brought on its own set of complications. The problem with my situationships was that they weren't beneficial to me in the long run. While I was focused on the short-term benefits, I didn't consider the long-term consequences. Although what I had with both men was based on convenience, for the men, it was the opposite—their relationships with me were based on dependence and *in*convenience. As the chapter reveals, scheming and using people just holds you back from your blessing. Nothing good really comes from being involved in one-sided relationships.

My experience, although negative, for the most part, showed me what I didn't want. And in this regard, it was beneficial. I had a decision to make—walk or remain in a meaningless state of being.

CHAPTER 17
Workbook Questions

1. Have you ever been in a situationship? Describe the situation.

....

....

....

....

....

....

....

2. What role did you play in the situationship?

....

....

....

....

....

....

....

3. Did you benefit anything from being involved in the situationship? What?

....

....

....

....

....

....

....

4. Do you regret being involved in the situationship? Would you ever do it again?

....

....

....

....

....

....

....

5. What did you learn from the situationship?

They That Wait

Recall Summary & Afterthought

We've heard it countless times … "Patience is a virtue" … "Good things come to those who wait." And the Bible even reminds us that "They that wait upon the Lord shall renew their strength" Isaiah 40:31. There's thousands of quotes and sayings about the power of patience and waiting for goodness to find you.

Chapter 18 is powerful because it challenges the notion that one must wait for a long time to receive a blessing or to see change take place in his or her life. We tend to believe we must endure great calamity or experience a lot of pain in order to receive God's greatest blessing. But as we see with my story, this isn't the case. Once I decided to end those one-sided relationships, it didn't take long for God to bring someone else—a man of integrity and valor—into my life. As we see, once God made up His mind, it was only a matter of three weeks before I met Cliché—the man God designed for me. And interestingly enough, I'd met him by pure happenstance. I didn't have to join an expensive dating site (although doing so is not highly discouraged); I didn't have to go to a club half-naked, I didn't have to lower my standards to be found by the person God designed especially for me.

As Chapter 18 shows us, blessings from God never come with huge price tags. You see, our experiences prepare us for the blessing. If we pay anything for blessings, payment comes in the form of blood, sweat, and tears—nonmonetary aspects. Getting out of my own way caused me to come in contact with my destiny sooner rather than later.

CHAPTER 18

Workbook Questions

1. Would you describe yourself as patient? Why or why not?

....

....

....

....

....

....

....

2. Are you patiently waiting (or have you patiently waited) for a blessing to occur in your life? Please give details.

....

....

....

....

....

....

....

3. How long did you have to wait, and why do you think you had to wait at all?

4. Was it worth it? How so?

Conflict of Interest

Recall Summary & Afterthought

I s it truly possible to have a conflict of interest in a personal matter? Yes, it definitely is possible, and Chapter 19 of my story shows us how. Trying to do things my way, in a way that would greatly benefit me, I became involved with two men, Jeff and Cliché. I was involved with one man, Jeff, for financial benefit, but when I met the handsome and charming Cliché, I wanted to end the relationship with Jeff. My only problem was I couldn't because I *needed* Jeff. Caught in a financial-dependency trap, I decided to do what so many people do—string Jeff along. This was where the conflict of interest arose.

As Chapter 19 reveals, conflicts of interest are not healthy. With this conflict of interest, Jeff and Cliché, whether they realized it or not, were competing with each another for my loyalty. But for me, my loyalty at that stage in my life was to sustenance and survival. I had to keep a roof over me and my children's heads. I had to keep food on the table. While both men expected me to have the best intentions when dealing with them, it was impossible for me to do so. And my inability to do so was the perfect illustration of how the very nature of a conflict of interest in relationships (especially romantic relationships) works. It inhibits one's ability to show loyalty toward one person over the other. This was the web I had spun for myself.

In this chapter, I began to pivot in terms of shifting my behavior in the right direction. I knew I had to make a change if I didn't want to lose out on the man I believed to be my true knight in shining armor.

Workbook Questions

1. Have you ever experienced a situation where there was a clear conflict of interest? Describe the situation.

....

....

....

....

....

....

....

2. How did you handle the conflict of interest?

....

....

....

....

....

....

....

....

3. Do you believe a conflict of interest imposes a moral dilemma? Why or why not?

....

....

....

....

....

....

....

4. How would you avoid becoming entangled in a conflict-of-interest scenario?

....

....

....

....

....

....

....

....

5. Is there ever a legitimate reason to become involved in a conflict of interest? Why or why not?

"Trauma is a fact of life. It does not,
however, have to be a life sentence."

~Peter A. Levine

Tug of War

Recall Summary & Afterthought

Just picture in your mind the game of tug of war. On each side, a team uses all their might and strength to knock their opponents off balance and pull them over the line of defeat. Chapter 20 shows us what the game tug of war looks like from a psychological point of view. The tug of war in this chapter was between Jeff and Cliché, with me standing in the middle. This triangular affair happens often. The danger with this scenario is that someone is always bound to get hurt. Usually, it's the person who is not ultimately chosen to remain in the relationship with the "love interest." In *Damaged Crowns Still Shine*, the love interest is me.

If you notice, outside of my involvement with men, my world was pretty empty, which set the precedent for the pattern I ultimately followed. One day, however, by happenstance, I bumped into an old friend by the name of Alisha. I knew Alisha from our days at an all-girl school. While reuniting with Alisha was an opportunity for me to begin developing and expanding my social circle, I was fearful of forming HEALTHY relationships. Do you now see the impact of trauma and dysfunctional relationships? They surround you like prison walls. And unbeknownst to me, it was the greatest dilemma that I had to, not only confront, but overcome.

The events that unfold in Chapter 20 serve as flashlights, shining on the dark areas of my life. As I held the flashlight, I was slowly becoming aware of the things around and within me that must change.

CHAPTER 20

Workbook Questions

1. Have you ever been involved in a relationship tug of war? Describe the situation.

....

....

....

....

....

....

....

2. What did you do?

....

....

....

....

....

....

....

....

3. If you could have done something differently, what would it have been?

....

....

....

....

....

....

....

4. What role does manipulation play in the relationship tug of war game? What parties are at fault?

....

....

....

....

....

....

....

5. To whom do you owe the greatest measure of honesty (besides God, The Creator, The Most High)?

Cliche

Recall Summary & Afterthought

Chapter 21 reminds me of a song that was first recorded by a man named Percy Sledge. The song was later recorded by Michael Bolton, for which it is most famously known. The song is, "When a Man Loves a Woman."

The song's lyrics capture Cliché's actions toward me. In his eyes, I was royalty. I was perfect and could do no wrong. Love is like shade; it hides the imperfections in people. For Cliché, I was the woman that he MUST marry. He came to me with his proposal of marriage, without me have to strong arm him into the idea of marrying me. Cliché simply came to my home with a plan already in place. The only things he needed from me were a "yes" and my signature on the marriage application and certificate.

For me, life had come full circle. All the pain and hurt from my childhood were like distant memories, and not because of Cliché himself, but because I had simply decided to move from my past into a future. I didn't check in with anyone—I didn't call my mother or ask for anyone else's opinion. It was all about moving forward with Cliché and a life that was not necessarily laced with rose petals but was shaped by commitment, loyalty, and unconditional love.

CHAPTER 21

Workbook Questions

1. Do you believe that you can experience a true love story? Why or why not?

....

....

....

....

....

....

....

2. Do you think it is wise to wait for love or go for it if it finds you?

....

....

....

....

....

....

....

3. Do you believe that love at first sight is such a thing? Why or why not?

4. Have you met your knight in shining armor? If so, how do you know?

5. Bonus Question: Do you believe I made the right decision to marry Cliché? Why or why not?

When All Hell Breaks Loose

Recall Summary & Afterthought

The phrase, "When all hell breaks loose," is used to describe what happens when violent, destructive, or chaotic activity suddenly occurs. And Chapter 22 captures it clearly.

If I even thought I'd have the love and support of my family after marrying Cliché, I was sadly mistaken. All it took was for me to make a Facebook announcement on my recent nuptials for all hell to break loose. And the reason all hell began to break loose in my life was because I'd dared to be independent and free myself from other people's control, opinions, and manipulation. To question another person's love is a clear tactic of manipulation, and that's what my mother did. The goal was to get me to question what I already knew to be true—that I was experiencing one of the purest forms of love, someone who loved me unconditionally.

When the manipulation didn't initially work, I was advised to consult the pastor to get his "permission." While it is wise to get the input or blessing of your spiritual leader, the spiritual leader must not abuse his or her authority. They must offer sound, unbiased advice that will breathe life into the new marriage, not confusion and discord.

Things seemed as though they were falling apart in my life. However, things were coming perfectly together. Breaking away from fear mongering, paranoia, self-sabotage, and manipulation only opened the door to a new life for me, one free of abuse, manipulation, and fear.

CHAPTER 22

Workbook Questions

1. Have you ever experienced a situation when you believed you should have been supported but you weren't? Describe the situation.

....

....

....

....

....

....

2. What did you learn from the experience?

....

....

....

....

....

....

....

3. How do you handle supporting a person or persons whose decisions you don't necessarily agree with?

4. Is there ever a reason to abandon someone because of their personal decision or decisions?

5. Do you feel you need approval to make decisions in your life? Explain.

....

....

....

....

....

....

....

....

....

6. When all hell breaks loose, do you face it or run?

....

....

....

....

....

....

....

....

....

Farewells and Good-Byes

Recall Summary & Afterthought

The final chapter in *Damaged Crowns Still Shine* is titled "Farewells and Good-Byes." These farewells and good-byes, however, are not about leaving people; they are about leaving circumstances behind. Throughout the book, we can see that I had my share of unfortunate events in my life. Yes, I was targeted. Yes, I was exploited. Yes, I was taken advantage of. Yes, all those things happened to me. But the important thing is that I did not wallow in my sorrow. I did not have a lasting pity party. Instead, time after time, I found a way to pick myself up. I didn't always get it right, but those detours from the track only helped me become a stronger person. I didn't have a choice because, not only did I have my children depending on me, but I had to depend on myself as well. That means I couldn't let myself down. Some things that happen in our lives are due to our decisions. Sometimes, we have a hand in our circumstances, and sometimes we don't—it's just life trying to teach us, mature us, and equip us for greater purpose.

Losing material things is nothing compared to losing your mind … your sanity … or, better yet, your belief in yourself. I couldn't afford to let myself down. I had enough fight within to rebuild myself … my life. The key to rebuilding your life is to forgive yourself for being naïve, vulnerable, or whatever the cause may be. When you are in a state of rebuilding, your sole focus should be on your intended or perceived outcome. How do you see yourself? What does your comeback story look like? If you create the proper space and appropriate time to rebuild yourself … your life, you will find that you have *no* time to worry, blame, lament in your sorrow, or complain. As the book revealed, I was focused on my vision to overcome homelessness and being exploited by family and so-called friends. I also made a commitment to myself to forgive, release, and let go of all attachments to any past struggles. This paved the way for me to be prepared for any future challenges, making me better not bitter. Thus, when I met Cliché, I was open to love and ready to both give and receive it.

The process of rebuilding helps us let go of all the pointless drama, all the toxic relationships, thoughts, and behaviors that are present in our lives, and keeps our focus away from the bad and on the good. Then, your motto, like mine will be "I'm better not bitter."

CHAPTER 23
Workbook Questions

1. Are you ready to say farewell and good-bye to the negative things in your life?

2. Do you have any drawbacks to leaving things and people behind if need be?

3. What will the NEW you and your NEW life look like?

"Change can be scary, but you know what's
scarier? Allowing fear to stop you
from growing, evolving, and progressing."

~Mandy Hale

Final Exercise

Are you ready to put the sparkle back into your life? Are you ready to replace those dull, damaged diamonds in your crown? Are you ready to hold your head up, despite the problems you've faced in your life? I'm sure you are!

For this final exercise, you'll need to purchase a lined journal. For the next 30 days, you will write about your growth or lack thereof in any of the areas covered in the workbook where you are struggling. After 30 days has elapsed, measure your growth again. In what ways have you addressed problem areas in your life? In what ways have you tried to tackle the problems? Did any of the measures work? How so? If not, why not? What do you think you can do differently to see growth or experience change in your life?

Repeat this process until all the diamonds in your crown have been replaced. Remember, just because you've experienced downfalls and setbacks in your life, it doesn't mean you should write your life (or even your loved one) off. Life is about growth and change, and change is inevitable.

1. What are the areas in your life where you would like to see personal growth or change?

....

....

....

....

....